Celebrate Martin Luther King Jr. Day

by Sally Lee

PEBBLE
a capstone imprint

First Facts are published by Pebble,
1710 Roe Crest Drive, North Mankato, Minnesota 56003
www.mycapstone.com

Library of Congress Cataloging-in-Publication Data
Library of Congress Cataloging-in-Publication data is available on the Library of Congress website.
ISBN 978-1-9771-0277-5 (library binding)
ISBN 978-1-9771-0533-2 (paperback)
ISBN 978-1-9771-0286-7 (eBook PDF)

Editorial Credits
Mandy Robbins, editor; Cynthia Della-Rovere, designer; Pam Mitsakos, media researcher;
Tori Abraham, production specialist

Photo Credits
AP Photo: Paul Sakuma, 14-15; Getty Images: Bettmann, 6 (bottom right); iStockphoto: asiseeit, Cover, SolStock, 20-21, Steve Debenport, 18-19; Newscom: CNP/Arnie Sachs, 11, Everett Collection, 7, National Archives via CNP, 5, ZUMA Press/White House, 12-13; Shutterstock: Bokeh Blur Background, Design Element, Duda Vasilii, Design Element, EPG_EuroPhotoGraphics, 3 (bottom left), 17, sharpner, 1 (bottom); The Image Works: ©Syracuse Newspapers, 8-9

Quote Citation
Page 2, excerpted from "The Drum Major Instinct," a sermon by Rev. Martin Luther King, Jr., 1968.

Printed and bound in the United States of America.
PA49

Table of Contents

Martin Luther King Jr.

Dr. Martin Luther King Jr. was a leader in the *civil rights* movement. In the 1950s and 1960s, he led millions of Americans to find peaceful ways to fight for equality. Americans honor his life and his work each year on the third Monday of January.

Fact Martin Luther King Jr. was born January 15, 1929. He grew up in Atlanta, Georgia. He became a minister like his father.

civil rights—the rights that all people have to be free and treated equally

King (right) speaks at a 1963 rally in Washington, D.C.

During King's life African-Americans had fewer rights than whites. Southern states had *segregation* laws. Blacks and whites could not use the same schools, bathrooms, or other public places. King led peaceful *protests* against these laws. The largest protest was the March on Washington.

Dr. King's Dream

In 1963 King helped lead the March on Washington. More than 250,000 people came to show their support for equal rights. At this march King gave his famous "I Have a Dream" speech. He dreamed of a country where everyone was treated equally.

There were even laws stating that whites and blacks had to drink from separate drinking fountains.

segregation—the practice of separating people according to groups, especially racial groups

protest—an action of a group of people who want something to be changed

The March on Washington convinced *Congress* to pass the Civil Rights Act in 1964. It outlawed segregation. President Lyndon B. Johnson signed the act into law. But King did not see all the results of his work. He was *assassinated* on April 4, 1968.

The news of King's death shocked the world.

Congress—the branch of a national government that makes laws

assassinate—to murder an important person

THE POST-STANDARD

SYRACUSE, N. Y., FRIDAY, APRIL 5, 1968

9, NO. 203

10 CENTS
60c Per Week Home Delivered

Chances of rain 20 per cent.
High today—48
Low tonight—30

TIN LUTHER KING SLAIN

...ing

...and Colder

...kles, colder temper-
...d strong winds are
...for today by the
...r Bureau. Partly
...es and cool temper-
...e predicted for to-
... The high tempera-
... will be 48 degrees,
... about 30. Chances of
...y are 20 per cent.
...ll be from the north-
... to 3s miles an hour.
...day's top temperature
... degrees, the low 48.
...an temperature was 56
... 21 degrees above last
... reading and 15 degrees
... normal.
...un will set at 6:35 p.m.
...nd rise at 5:38 a.m. to-
...ow. Vehicular lamps
...e lighted by 7:05 p.m.

...ought for Today

...ould rather be right than
...esident — Henry Clay,
...can Statesman (177-

Shows Where Shot Hit

The Rev. Andrew Young, an aide to Dr. Martin
Luther King, shows where Dr. King was hit by an
assassin's bullet in Memphis, Tenn., last night.
Young was pictured in the emergency room of St.
Joseph's Hospital. (AP Wirephoto).

LBJ Says America Shocked

WASHINGTON (AP) — President Johnson spoke Thursday night of an "America shocked and saddened" by the assassination of Dr. Martin Luther King as he condemned violence, lawlessness and divisiveness.

In a brief, solemn message to the nation, Johnson disclosed that because of the slaying at Memphis he had canceled plans for a political appearance Thursday night and postponed until Friday his scheduled midnight departure for Hawaii and a Vietnam strategy conference.

The President appeared in the doorway of the White House offices, stern-faced and spoke on all television and radio networks.

"I ask every American citizen," he said, "to reject the blind violence that has struck down Dr. King, who lived by nonviolence."

The President urged prayers for peace and understanding in the land and said:

"We can achieve nothing by lawlessness and divisiveness among the American people."

He said he hopes all Americans would search their hearts.

At that point he said he was cancelling all plans for the evening and postponing until Friday his planned take-off for Hawaii and conferences there on problems of war and peace in Vietnam.

He was to have attended a Democratic fund-raising dinner at a Washington Hotel Thursday night and was only minutes from leaving the White House when the tragic news came from Memphis.

The White House said Johnson had telephoned Mrs. King at her home in Atlanta and expressed his sympathy.

The text of President Johnson's statement:

"America is shocked and saddened by the brutal slaying tonight of Dr. Martin Luther King.

"I ask every American to reject the blind violence that has struck Dr. King who lived by nonviolence.

"I pray that his family can find comfort in the memory of all he tried to do for the land he loved so well. I have just conveyed the sympathy of Mrs.

DR. MARTIN LUTHER KING JR.
Civil Rights Leader Assassinated

Associated Press Wirephoto

U.S. Leaders Deplore Killing

NEW YORK (AP) — The nation's civil rights and political leaders reacted with anguish, shock and grief Thursday night at the slaying of the Rev. Dr. Martin Luther King Jr. in Memphis.

There also was fear that the slaying could lead to more violence.

"We have been saddened," President Johnson told the nation on radio and television. "I ask every citizen to reject the blind violence that has struck Dr. King who lived in nonviolence.

The President said he was postponing his trip to Hawaii, for a Vietnam strategy conference, until Friday. He had been scheduled to leave about midnight Thursday.

Vice President Hubert H. Humphrey said the slaying "brings shame to our country. An apostle of nonviolence has been the victim of violence."

The vice president said, however, that his death will bring new strength to the cause he fought for.

A spokesman for the National Association for the Advancement of Colored People said, "I am shocked and grieved by this wanton violence of a peace-loving man, a dedicated, courageous man. This murder certainly does not solve anything and it will be deeply resented by Negroes through the country and by other people who believe in nonviolent protest."

Former Vice President Rich-

State Flags Ordered At Half Staff

NEW YORK (9P)—Gov. Nelson A. Rockefeller ordered flags on all state buildings flown at half-staff Friday "as an expression of the deep sorrow felt by New Yorkers" at the death of Dr. Martin Luther King, Jr.

In a statement, the governor said Dr.

Police Nab 2 in Hunt For Killer

MEMPHIS, Tenn. (AP) — Nobel Laureate Martin Luther King Jr., father of non-violence in the American Civil rights movement, was killed by an assassin's bullet Thursday night.

King, 39, was hit in the neck by a bullet as he stood on the balcony of a motel here. He died less than an hour later in St. Joseph Hospital.

Gov. Buford Ellington immediately ordered 4,000 National Guard troops back into the city. A curfew, which was clamped on Memphis after a King-led march turned into a riot a week ago, was reimposed.

Police said incidents of violence, including several fire bombings were reported following King's death.

The 1964 Nobel Peace Prize winner, was standing on the balcony of his motel here, where he had come to lead protests in behalf of the city's 1,300 striking garbage workers, most of them Negroes, when he was shot.

Two unidentified men were arrested several blocks from the motel.

Police also said they found a 30-06 rifle on Main Street about one block from the motel, but it was not confirmed whether this was the weapon that killed King.

An aide who was standing nearby said the shot hit King in the neck and lower right part of his face.

"Martin Luther King is dead," said Asst. Police Chief Henry Lux, the first word of the death.

Asst. Hospital Administrator Paul Hess confirmed later that King died at 7 p.m. of a bullet wound in the neck.

The Rev. Jesse Jackson said he and others in the King party were getting ready to go to dinner when the shooting occurred.

"King was on the second floor balcony of the motel," Jackson said. "He had just bent over. If he had been standing up, he wouldn't have been hit in the face."

King had just told Ben Branch: "My man, be sure to sing 'Blessed Lord' tonight and sing it well."

A shot then rang out, the only sound Jackson said.

...ohnson Defers Trip ...fter Murder of Dr. King

...SHINGTON (AP) — Presi-...
Johnson, preparing for a
... Vietnam strategy
...rence in Honolulu, delayed
...departure overnight Thurs-
... because of the assassination
... Memphis of the Rev. Dr.
... Luther King.
...he President went before
...vision cameras and radio
...rophones to declare Ameri-
... is "shocked and saddened"
... the tragedy. He condemned

...violence, lawlessness and divisiveness.

Johnson goes to Honolulu Sunday to meet in Hawaii with former President, dent, Chung Hee Park.

Earlier in the day, Hanoi charged that American planes bombed a North Vietnamese town northwest of the country's capital—deep inside the territory the President had declared off limits to U.S. air raiders.

The Pentagon quickly disavowed any "present knowledge of any such U.S. attack since the President's speech, Sunday night" in which he proclaimed the curtailment of U.S. bombing of North Vietnam.

"Nonetheless an immediate investigation has been ordered," Asst. Secretary Phil G. Goulding said in issuing the De-

John on also to meet in Hawaii Sunday with South Korea's president,

The White House did not indicate whether Johnson would change his earlier plan to meet at March Air Force Base, Calif., to talk with former President Dwight D. Eisenhower.

The original plan called for

King was saddened by the brutal slaying tonight of Dr. Martin Luther King.

Mrs. King and myself to his wid-

President Hailed ... St. Patrick's

Creating a Holiday

Efforts to make a holiday honoring King began four days after his death. U.S. Congressman John Conyers introduced a bill to create a national holiday. Lawmakers voted against it. Some didn't want a holiday for a private citizen. Others didn't think King deserved a holiday.

Early Celebrations

Coretta Scott King didn't want people to forget her husband. She planned the first event to celebrate his birthday in 1969. Four years later, Illinois made Martin Luther King Jr. Day a holiday. It was the first state to do so. Massachusetts and Connecticut followed in 1974.

Coretta Scott King gives a speech in Washington, D.C., in 1968.

In 1983 more than 500,000 people gathered in Washington, D.C. It was the 20th anniversary of the March on Washington. Six million people had signed *petitions* asking Congress to make a holiday for King. The bill passed that year. President Ronald Reagan signed it into law.

petition—a written document that people sign to show that they want a person or organization to do something

President Ronald Reagan signs the paperwork to make Martin Luther King Jr. Day a national holiday.

Celebrations

The first national Martin Luther King Jr. Day was held on January 20, 1986. Atlanta, Georgia, had the biggest celebration. People came to march with the King family. Only 17 states held celebrations the first year. By 2000 all 50 states did.

Local leaders march in San Francisco's first Martin Luther King Jr. Day celebration.

Many schools and government offices are closed on Martin Luther King Jr. Day. Families celebrate by going to parades, picnics, and church services. Some cities have concerts and speeches honoring King.

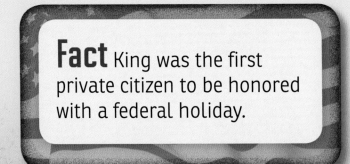

Fact King was the first private citizen to be honored with a federal holiday.

King's life was spent serving others. To honor his work, a change was made to his holiday. Congress made it a national day of service in 1994. Now many *volunteers* spend the day helping out in their communities.

Fact King once said, "Everybody can be great because anybody can serve."

volunteer—a person who does work without getting paid for it

People can honor King by serving others and fighting for equality. They can help those in need and clean up public places. People can also speak up when others are being treated unfairly. They can continue the work of a man who died trying to make the world better for others.

Glossary

assassinate (us-SASS-uh-nate)—to murder an important person

civil rights (SI-vil RYTS)—the rights that all people have to be free and treated equally

Congress (KAHNG-gruhs)—the branch of a national government that makes laws

petition (puh-TISH-uhn)—a written document that people sign to show that they want a person or organization to do something

protest (pro-TEST)—an action of a group of people who want something to be changed

segregation (seg-ruh-GAY-shuhn)—the practice of separating people according to groups, especially racial groups

volunteer (vol-uhn-TIHR)—a person who does work without getting paid to do it

Read More

Hooks, Gwendolyn. *If You Were a Kid During the Civil Rights Movement.* If You Were a Kid. New York: Children's Press, an imprint of Scholastic Inc., 2017.

Koestler-Grack, Rachel A. *Martin Luther King, Jr. Day.* Celebrating Holidays. Minneapolis: Bellwether Media, Inc., 2018.

Weakland, Mark. *When Martin Luther King Jr. Wore Roller Skates.* Leaders Doing Headstands. North Mankato, Minn.: Picture Window Books, 2017.

Internet Sites

Use FactHound to find Internet sites related to this book.

Visit www.facthound.com

Just type in 9781977102775 and go.

Check out projects, games and lots more at
www.capstonekids.com

Critical Thinking Questions

1. Martin Luther King Jr. had a dream. What did he want to see happen?
2. How can you celebrate Martin Luther King Jr. Day?
3. What was one change that came about because of Martin Luther King Jr.'s efforts?

Index